Héritier NAHANO KALEMBIRE

National Accounting Course 1st Edition

Héritier NAHANO KALEMBIRE

National Accounting Course 1st Edition

Courses for students in economics and political science

ScienciaScripts

Cover image: www.ingimage.com

This book is a translation from the original published under ISBN 978-620-2-53203-7.

Publisher:
Sciencia Scripts
is a trademark of
International Book Market Service Ltd., member of OmniScriptum Publishing Group
17 Meldrum Street, Beau Bassin 71504, Mauritius
Printed at: see last page
ISBN: 978-620-2-58974-1

CONTENT PAGE

INTRODUCTION

It is possible to describe the functioning of an economy in different ways:

- by giving priority to the study of the behaviour of each individual agent, producer or consumer, this is the perspective of *microeconomics* ;
- considering the functioning of the economic system as a whole (Keynesian view), this is the view of *macroeconomics*.

National accountants have chosen the macroeconomic perspective by presenting in a rigorous and coherent framework all the economic operations carried out each year by the various agents making up the nation. This is an essential instrument for collecting and recording quantifiable data that can be applied to very different areas and economic units. Understanding this information system, which is more or less elaborate, means, on the one hand, defining what is meant by economic agents and specifying the operations they carry out, and, on the other hand, giving a conventional representation of the national accounts.

Thus, national accounting is a "*comprehensive, detailed and quantified representation of the national economy within an accounting framework*".

Its main purpose is to collect and organise statistical information, to represent economic circuits, to evaluate aggregates, etc. These tools enable the analysis of economic and financial behaviour and the results of economic policy.

CHAPTER 1. THE ECONOMIC CIRCUIT

The national accounts' representation of economic reality is that of the circuit. It is in fact a matter of presenting the relationships (in the form of transactions) that exist between the various economic agents. In the case of an economy with two agents (households and firms), the circuit describes how firms simultaneously create goods and services (real flows) and income (cash flows). These incomes are received by households in exchange for factors of production (land, labour, or capital) that they have provided to firms and which constitute a real flow. Households spend part of their income by purchasing goods and services produced by firms (this is called consumption) and keep the other part in the form of savings.

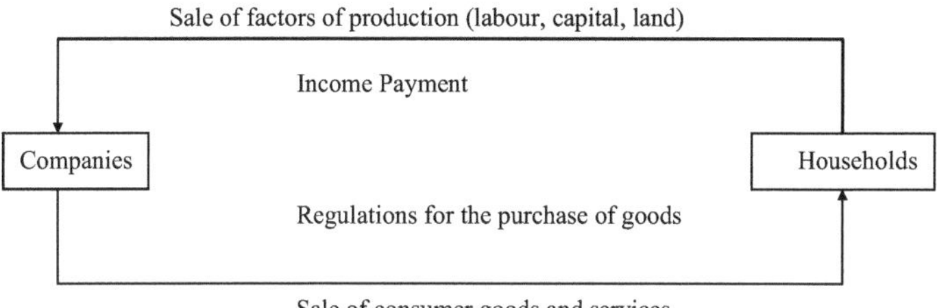

I.1. CLOSED ECONOMY CIRCUIT

I.1.1 Two-agent circuit

In a closed economy, restricted to two agents (households and enterprises), the national accounts present economic transactions in the following way. Households use part of their income to buy the goods sold by the firm, C, and the other part to save, S. Their income, R, can thus be broken down as follows: R = C + S. Firms, for their part, will be able to produce, Y, thanks to the investments they have previously made, I. Firms produce consumer goods C but also production goods (machinery, etc.) I. Let Y = C + I. Therefore, for there to be **economic equilibrium** (supply = demand) and for the circuit to be completed, savings must be equal to investment, i.e. S = I. The diagram below shows the transactions carried out between households and enterprises.

I.1.2 Overall circuit of the national economy

When one moves from an economy with two agents to the whole national economy, the circuit becomes somewhat more complex through the integration of Financial Institutions and Administrations.

- The role of Financial Institutions is to act as a financial intermediary between businesses and households. They intervene on two major economic variables: investment and savings. Firms can finance their investments through *self-financing* (depreciation plus retained earnings), but also through *credit (*in which case the firm will have to pay interest to the banks) or through the *financial market* (issues of securities: shares, bonds). Households can use their savings to acquire *monetary assets* (banknotes, coins, term deposits), *financial assets* (securities issued on the financial market by companies) or *real assets* (gold, silver, real estate, etc.). Households' savings are generally remunerated in the form of interest by banks.
- Administrations such as the State, local authorities and Social Security, finance their Public Expenditure (PE) through compulsory levies (Taxation, Social Contributions) that affect households and companies. Public Expenditure enables governments to purchase goods and services from businesses (equipment, materials, etc.), to pay salaries to households (e.g. civil servants), to have businesses carry out major works (public works, roads, etc.), and to make transfers to economic agents who need them (family allowances for households, subsidies for businesses, etc.). In the event that the compulsory levies are not sufficient to cover public expenditure, we speak of a *budget deficit* (it should be noted that one of the characteristics of administrations is a chronic need for financing). In this case, governments must finance themselves by issuing securities on the financial market (Treasury bills, bonds) or by resorting to bank credit.

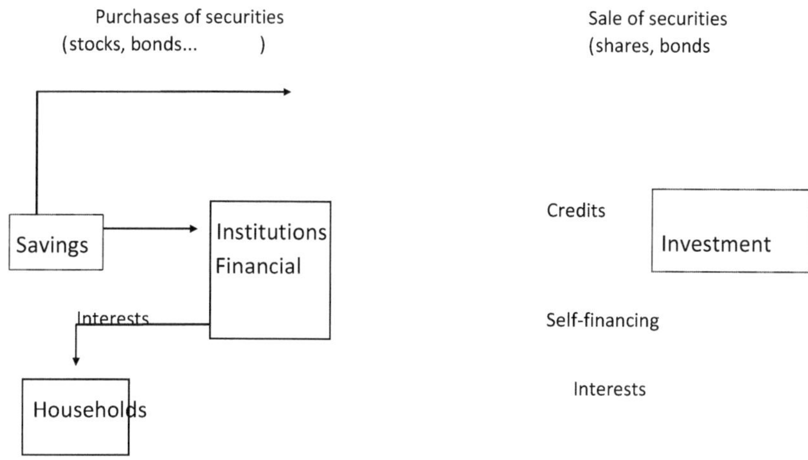

Distribution of sala ires, dividends, interest

I. 2. OPEN ECONOMY CIRCUIT

In an open economy, you have to bring in the rest of the world. The relations between a national economy and the rest of the world are not limited to exports (counted as a job: it is the use of a certain production) and imports (counted as a resource: especially when national production is insufficient in relation to demand). The rest of the world and the domestic economy are closely linked through the development of international financial markets and the many connections established within financial institutions.

As the various national economies are increasingly dependent on the outside world, it is possible to measure this dependence *by calculating a dependency ratio*. The latter is equivalent to the sum of imports and exports relative to GDP (wealth created by the nation). It can be noted, however, that the interdependence between various economies can be of a very different nature depending on whether the trade is in products, capital, goods or services.....

Purchases of goods and services: Consumption

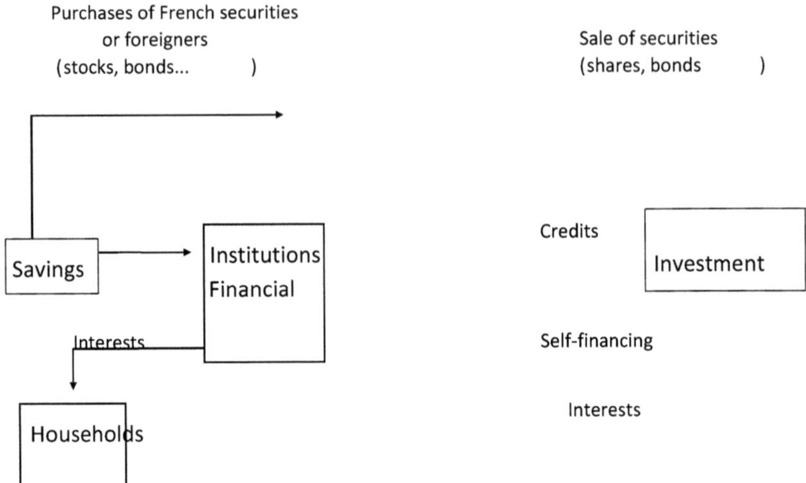

Distribution of salaries, dividends, interest

CHAPTER 2. PRESENTATION OF NATIONAL ACCOUNTS

National accounts are a "*comprehensive, detailed and quantified representation of the national economy within an accounting framework*". It lists most of the information and economic concepts that can be used to analyse the national economy. The national accounts summarise the transactions carried out by economic agents in accounts (uses - resources).

II.1 ECONOMIC AGENTS

National accounts generally use institutional breakdown to represent all economic agents. These are then referred to as *institutional units*. These are centres of economic decision-making, meeting in principle the following two criteria:

(i) they enjoy autonomy of decision in the exercise of their main function;

(ii) they have a complete set of accounts, with a balance sheet.

Institutional units are grouped into institutional sectors. *An institutional sector is a set of institutional units that behave in a similar economic manner*. This economic behaviour is identified by the main function, nature and source of resources of the institutional unit.

The national accounts distinguishes 6 institutional sectors :

1. Non-financial corporations and quasi-corporations (SQS)

This institutional sector comprises institutional units whose main function is to produce marketable (i.e. economically significant priced) non-financial goods and services and whose resources are derived from the proceeds of their sales. This sector includes *companies with full accounting records and legal personality*. Their legal forms are varied: public limited company, limited liability company, general partnership, etc. It also includes *quasi-corporations* (which have full accounting records but do not have legal personality). Their economic importance is such (they are branches, sales offices, companies in the head office is abroad) that they are described together with the companies. On the other hand, sole proprietorships, which do not have a legal personality separate from that of the entrepreneur, are excluded from this institutional sector[1]. Non-financial corporations are grouped into three sectors according to the nature of the control exercised: *public non-financial corporations* (controlled by the State or by local authorities, they are legally public administrations, but they sell most of their output to the public, e.g. régideso); *domestic private non-financial corporations* (they are managed on behalf of partners, linked by a company contract) and *foreign-controlled non-financial corporations*. Another, more traditional, breakdown classifies companies according to their main activity. A distinction is thus made between the concepts of branch (activity of a company) and sector (main activity of a company). Industry studies provide a picture of product markets in the form of an IOT (input-output table). Sector studies facilitate the analysis of variables such as investment, financing, etc.

[1] Sole proprietorships (farmers, small-scale industrialists, craftsmen, tradesmen, professionals), which sell non-financial goods and services, are considered by the national accounts as households.

2. Financial companies

This sector comprises the institutional units whose main function is to finance, i.e. to collect, transform and distribute financial resources. Their role is to link agents in need of finance (seeking funds) with agents in a position to finance (willing to invest funds). They are engaged in financial intermediation. The resources of credit institutions are made up of the funds they collect: demand or time deposits, bonds, etc. The sector breaks down into three sub-sectors.

- *The financial institutions* grouping together the institutions that have the power to create money. They include the central bank (which has a monopoly on issuing legal tender); other deposit-taking institutions (second-tier banks that create book money); and other financial intermediaries.

- *Financial auxiliaries* (MasterCard Group...).

- *Insurance companies* (including mutual *insurance companies*, institutions whose resources are voluntary social contributions). The main function of insurance companies is to transform individual risks into collective risks, by guaranteeing the payment of compensation if a risk materialises. Their resources are the premiums paid by policyholders under voluntary contracts.

3. Households

This sector comprises institutional units whose main function is to consume goods and services purchased on the market. By including the individual entrepreneur in households, the system of national accounts has created an institutional sector with very heterogeneous behaviour[2]. **The** main resources of households come from the remuneration of factors of production (labour, capital, land) and transfers from other sectors. Within households, a distinction is made between *ordinary households* (set of persons living in separate or independent housing) and *collective households* (retirement homes, university halls of residence, workers' hostels, prisons). In order to enable a better analysis of economic behaviour, a breakdown by Occupations and Socio-professional Categories of households is regularly published. This categorisation is thus used to classify households according to the occupation of the household reference person. The breakdown of households is based on the intersection of several criteria: the activity criterion (which separates the active from the inactive), the status criterion (which separates the self-employed, whether employees or not, and salaried employees), the sector of activity criterion (which separates agriculture from other activities), the hierarchical criterion (which combines income, diploma and the notion of management).

4. General government

This sector covers all units whose main function is to produce non-market services for all units or to carry out operations for the redistribution of income or national wealth. In other words, they provide free or quasi-free collective services and redistribute national income. The main resources are compulsory levies: taxes, social contributions. This sector is divided into three sub-sectors: *central public administration (APUC),* essentially comprising the State and bodies

[2] The productive activity of sole proprietorships is carried out within an economic unit which does not have a legal personality distinct from the natural personality of its holder. As a result, the assets of the enterprise and those of the household are confused. And the operations relating to the professional activity are not always distinct from those relating to the domestic activity.

with general or specialised competence; *local public administrations (APUL),* comprising local authorities with general competence extended to part of the territory (regions, departments, communes) and various local government bodies with specialised competence (régies, districts, chamber of commerce, etc.); *social security administrations,* comprising all the units that collect compulsory social contributions and distribute social benefits, and the bodies to which these units provide their main resources (hospitals).

5. Non-profit institutions serving households (NPISHs)

They include private non-profit organizations producing non-market services for households. They are mainly associations, trade unions, political parties, churches, etc. They have legal personality. Their resources come from voluntary contributions from households and property income for more than 50% of their income. If more than 50% of their revenues come from sales, non-profit organizations can be classified as corporations. If more than 50% of their revenues come from government grants, they are classified as general government.

6. The Rest of the World

It is a grouping of relations between foreign and domestic economic units. It is therefore not a true institutional sector. The rest of the world is broken down by geographical location.

Table 1: Institutional Sector Resources and Functions

Institutional Sector	**Main Function**	**Key Resources**
SQS and SQS NF	Producing non-financial market goods and services	Result of the sale
Financial companies	To finance, i.e. to collect, transform and distribute available funds.	Funds from financial commitments entered into.
Households (including sole proprietorships)	Consumers, and as individual entrepreneurs, produce non-financial market goods and services.	Factor compensation, transfers from other sectors, proceeds from sales.
Administrations Public	Producing non-market services for the community and carrying out operations for the redistribution of income and national wealth.	Mandatory payments made by other sectors and received directly or indirectly.
Non-Profit Institutions Serving Households (NPISHs)	Producing non-market services and in some cases producing, on a non-profit basis, market services for households.	Voluntary contributions made by households, and possibly purchases of goods by households.
The Rest of the World	Under the heading "Rest of the World", transactions between resident and non-resident units are grouped in the same set of accounts.	

II.2 ECONOMIC OPERATIONS

All economic acts are aggregated here into a small number of transactions with a certain degree of homogeneity. These transactions can be grouped into three categories according to the nature of the economic activity under consideration: transactions in goods and services, distributive transactions and financial transactions.

1. Transactions in goods and services

These operations indicate on the one hand the *origin of the goods and services used on the* national territory (i.e. the resources available to the economy), i.e. production (P) and imports (IMP), and on the other hand *their final use*. There are generally six such uses: intermediate consumption (IC), final consumption (FC), gross fixed capital formation (GFCF), changes in stocks (VS) and exports (EXP). We will successively study these eight transactions on goods and services.

a. Consumption

It is broken down into intermediate consumption and final consumption expenditure (FC). *Intermediate consumption* (IC) *represents the value of market goods and services destroyed in the various production processes*. It differs from final consumption because it is productive consumption. It also differs from gross fixed capital formation in that it relates to goods whose life span is shorter than the annual period. It is possible to separate external intermediate consumption (consumption by one industry of products from another industry) from intra-consumption (intermediate consumption of products from the industry itself, e.g. oil consumed by a refinery).

Final consumption expenditure (FC) *represents the value of goods and services used for the direct satisfaction of individual or collective needs*. It is assumed that goods are not stored but consumed at the time of purchase, even when they are durable (e.g. the purchase of a car or a television set). The purchase of housing receives special treatment, as it is associated with an investment (gross fixed capital formation).

As household final consumption expenditure is too restrictive (it excludes consumption expenditure that benefits households but is borne by the community or public administration, for example education or health), national accounts now distinguish between *final consumption expenditure (*FCE) and *actual final consumption* (EC). Actual final consumption (EC) of households is equal to the sum of their final consumption expenditure and individualised consumption (this includes expenditure on education and health borne by the administration[3]). For actual final consumption to be higher than final consumption expenditure, income must be higher than the gross disposable income of households. For this, it is sufficient to consider that the government transfers additional income (social benefits) to households.

b. Gross fixed capital formation

That's the name given to the investment. GFCF is defined as *the value of acquisitions (net of disposals) of fixed assets by resident producers*. The acquisition is not necessarily a purchase, it can be the result of production for own final use (e.g. an enterprise producing software for itself). The asset is fixed because it can be used continuously and repeatedly for more than one year. Fixed assets can be either tangible or intangible. Tangible assets include machinery, dwellings, buildings, civil engineering works (bridges, roads, etc.) and the value of major repairs to these assets. Intangible assets include software acquisitions, mining and oil exploration expenditures, ... The GFCF of households that are not sole proprietors concerns

[3] They do not include expenditures related to defence, general administration or other functions that benefit the community as a whole.

only the acquisition of new dwellings or major repairs to existing dwellings. The national accounts exclude from GFCF the intensity of research and development, which nevertheless has positive effects on production for several years.

c. Changes in inventories

Inventories *include all goods with a life of less than one year held at any one time by resident producer units.* Inventories are products held for future use or sale. In the flow accounts, the national accounts record only the changes in stocks during the year and not their amount. By convention, neither households nor non-market branches of government hold stocks. The change in stocks (noted VS) represents the difference between stock entries and stock withdrawals, valued at market prices on the day of the transaction. The change in stocks is valued at purchaser prices, excluding deductible VAT such as GFCF.

d. Production

According to the National Accounts, production is *the economic activity of creating goods and services that are usually traded on the market from factors of production that are traded on the market.* To study production, it is preferable to use units of homogeneous production rather than institutional sectors. Just as institutional units are grouped into institutional sectors, homogeneous production units are grouped into branches. Output (P) is broken down into market output (MP), own final use output (OFE) and other non market output (ONP).

- *Market Production* (MP): Production is market when it is traded or is likely to be traded on a market, at a price that can be considered as at least covering the costs of production. The evaluation of the production of market goods and services is therefore done at the market price (base price). All goods are conventionally considered to be market goods. However, some goods are not intended to be sold; these are those which the producer reserves for his own use, either as intermediate consumption, final consumption or own-account production of fixed capital goods.

- *Own final use production (OFP)* is production for final consumption or GFCF of the producing agent (85% is attributable to households). Finally, production for own final use covers self-consumed agricultural production.

- *Other non-market output* (ONP) is defined as output that "*is supplied to other units either free of charge or at an economically insignificant price*" (i.e. covers less than half of the production costs). Some services are indeed non-market. They cannot be sold on a market because they are indivisible (defence, police, street lighting, etc.) or are sold at a very low price out of political will and because they generate positive externalities (education). In the absence of market prices, these non-market services are valued by the sum of their production costs: compensation of employees (civil servants), products used as intermediate consumption to produce these services, taxes linked to production, consumption of fixed capital. The national accounts consider that the resources constituted by non-market services (NMS) are used as final consumption expenditure by households for the amount of their partial payments (university fees, etc.) and as final consumption expenditure by governments (individual or collective expenditure).

If one wants to measure the mass of goods and services obtained from the production process with a single figure, it is necessary to weight the elementary quantities produced by prices, but also to avoid counting the same products several times. Indeed, finished goods (more elaborate) are generally made from more rudimentary goods (raw materials, semi-finished products, etc.). The value of these goods (*intermediate consumption*) **is** part of the price of the finished goods they are used to produce. Hence there is a risk of double counting, if the prices of the various products are added together without precaution (if the value of automobile production and the value of windscreen production are recorded, double counting occurs since the price of the windscreen is included in the price of the automobile). To avoid such double counting, the value of intermediate consumption at each stage of the production process should be subtracted from the value of the product at each stage of the production process in order to obtain value added.

Either Production - intermediate consumption = Value added

The sum of value added at all stages of the production process gives the *gross domestic product* (GDP). GDP is the aggregate representing the mass of goods and services produced by resident units and made available to final users.

e. Operations with the rest of the world

Exports (EXP) represent the value of goods and services provided by resident units to non-resident units. *Imports* (**IMP)** refers to the provision of goods and services by the rest of the world to the domestic economy. Domestic agents may then consume foreign products in this way. Exports are valued Free on Board (FOB)[4]. They are valued exclusive of VAT. Imports are valued CIF ([5]cost, insurance, freight), i.e. their FOB value at the border of the exporting country. Exports and imports of market services include transport, insurance, communication and other services valued at market prices.

The accounting balance of a product's **resources and uses is** written as follows:

$$P + IMP = CI + DF + FBCF \pm VS + EXP$$

However, this equation can still be improved by making certain adjustments :

- Since the value actually created by the company is equal to production minus intermediate consumption, the value added is then obtained. The sum of the added values gives the **Gross Domestic Product** (GDP).
- Gross Fixed Capital Formation (GFCF) is generally equal to an investment (I) made over several periods by economic agents. Hence GFCF = **I**
- Final consumption expenditure (FC) is associated with the household consumption function. It is denoted as consumption (C)

The new general job-resource balance can be written as follows:

$$GDP + IMP = C + I \pm VS + EXP$$

[4] At FOB price, i.e. the price understood to be the price for goods delivered on board the vessel, with all costs, duties, taxes and risks borne by the seller until the goods reach their destination.

[5] At the CIF price, i.e. the price understood for goods arriving at the port of destination, with freight paid and insurance covered.

Gross domestic product (GDP) is thus the sum of domestic demand (C + I ± VS) and foreign demand (EXP - IMP).

2. Allocation operations

They describe the formation and flow of income. They show how income circulates between economic agents prior to receiving a final job. While transactions in goods and services are the beginning and end of the circuit, distributive transactions - like financial transactions - are the intermediate links.

a. Classification of income distribution transactions

- *Compensation of employees* includes all cash payments and benefits provided in kind by employers as compensation for work. This is broken down into gross wages and salaries; employers' actual social contributions and notional social contributions (these represent the counterpart of social benefits provided directly, outside any contribution circuit, by employers to their employees, e.g. the maintenance of full pay even in the event of sickness).

- *Taxes related to production and imports*: these are compulsory levies by general government on the production and import of goods and services. They include VAT on products[6], other taxes linked to production (this not very homogeneous category includes, for example, customs duties, etc.), and other taxes linked to production.
- *Operating subsidies*: these are current transfers paid by governments to producing units with the aim of lowering the price of their products and/or allowing sufficient remuneration of the factors of production.

- *Property and business income*: these transactions trace the distribution of part of the gross operating surplus. They are recorded in the income accounts and include interest and remuneration on certain debts; income from land (renting, sharecropping) and intangible assets; dividends and other distributed income from corporations; income collected by entrepreneurs of quasi-corporations; and employee participation in the fruits of the expansion of the enterprise.

- *Property and casualty insurance operations* include net property and casualty insurance premiums and claims

- *Unquoted current transfers* include current taxes on income and wealth (income tax, personal income tax, local taxes, vignette paid by households, etc.); actual social contributions paid either by insured persons or by their employees; notional social contributions (counterpart of social benefits provided directly by employers to their employees); social benefits; current transfers between general government (transfer of tax revenue); current transfers to NPISHs; current international cooperation; private international transfers (e.g. transfer of migrants' remittances) and miscellaneous current transfers.

3. Financial operations

In the legal sense, they relate to financial rights that take the name of *claims* when considered from the point of view of their holder and *debts* if one sits on the side of the obliged party. Financial transactions are transactions that reflect changes in the receivables and payables of

---

[6] Value added tax is collected by companies who charge it to their customers. They do not pay all the invoiced VAT to the state, as usually part of the invoiced VAT is deductible. The VAT charged on products is therefore equal to the difference between the invoiced VAT and the deductible VAT. It is entered as a resource in the general government revenue account. However, it does not appear in the use of any account.

the sectors. They are the counterpart of transactions in goods and services, distributive transactions, or pure financial transactions. For the national accounts, currency is a claim on the holder of the currency and a liability for the credit institution that issued it. Financial transactions show how sectors that spent more than their resources went into debt, and how those that spent less than their resources used that surplus. The financial transactions show how this offsetting took place between the sectors with a financing need and those with a financing capacity. It is the financial transactions tables (FOTs) which, by describing the movements of currency and other claims, show how financial equilibrium is achieved.

The financial transactions table shows the relationship between the institutional sectors shown in the columns and the financial transactions shown in the rows. The six sectors, the net flows of debts and the net flows of receivables are shown. The balances of receivables and payables reflect the financing needs and capacities of the various sectors. The TOF shows how the institutional sectors have used their financing capacity or met their financing needs. The TOF can be used for a comparative study of financial systems, both in time and space. It can also be used to inform credit policy (the art of manipulating the range of investment and financing instruments) by varying their form and cost.

II.3 INSTITUTIONAL SECTOR ACCOUNTS

By aggregating goods and services transactions and distributive transactions, an account can be obtained for each institutional sector. For each sector account, a **resource** is defined as any transaction that represents an inflow of money, and a **use is** defined as any transaction that represents an outflow of money. Like all accounts, the national accounts present accounts in balance, by writing the balance, **capacity or need for financing, within the** accounts of this sector.

If Resource > to Jobs = Financing Capacity. And if Resource < Jobs = Need for funding.

0. The Global Accounts

Compte global des entreprises

Emplois	**Ressources**
Achat des Matières Premières	Ventes des produits
Intérêts payés par les entreprises	Subventions reçues
Salaires payés par les entreprises	Intérêts reçus
Intérêts payés par les entreprises	
Impôts payés	

Compte Global des Ménages

Emplois	**Ressources**
Achat des Biens et Services	Salire reçu
Impôts sur salaire	Transfert reçu
Transfert effectué	Intérêts reçu
intérêts payés	Profit

Compte de l'Administration Publique

Emplois	**Ressources**
Achat des Biens et Services	Impôts reçus
Subvention accordée	Cotisations
Salaire payé	Intérêts reçus
Intérêts payés	Transferts reçus
Transferts effectués	

Compte du reste du Monde

Emplois	**Ressources**
Importation	Exportation
Salaire frontalier envoyé	Transferts reçus
Transfert effectué	

1. Accounts by Transaction

Between the different institutional sectors, three types of operation can be distinguished:

- *The operation on products*: describes the origin and use of goods and services in the economy.
- *The redistribution operation*: retrace the distribution and redistribution of income from production or relations with the rest of the world.
- *The financial transaction*: relates to receivables and payables.

The transactions of each sector are grouped into 5 current accounts and 2 accumulation accounts.

- 5 current accounts: these are kept as employment/resources and describe the nature, origin and use of income over a period of time. They are :

- Production account
- Operating Account
- Allocation of primary income account
- Secondary Income Distribution Account
- Use of Income Account

• 2 accumulation accounts: these are kept as changes in assets/liabilities and describe the change in net wealth over a period. They are :

- Capital Account
- Financial account

The accounts are linked because the balance of each account appears as a resource in the next account. The breakdown of activity into accounts should make it possible to show different balances that are relevant to economic analysis.

1°). NON-FINANCIAL COMPANY OR ENTERPRISE

✓ **The production account**

It only includes transactions on products. The balance is Gross Value Added (GVA). This value added represents the productive contribution of the sector to the economy.

This account has the same structure for all sectors.

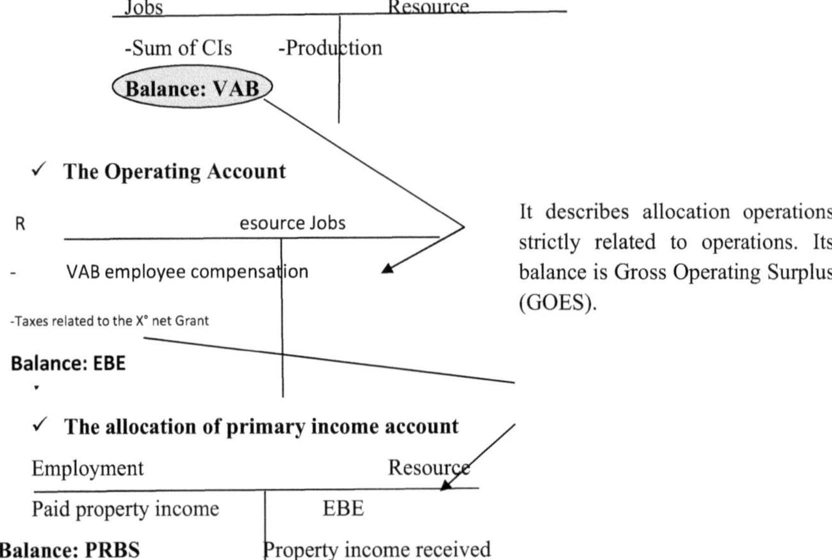

It includes only allocation transactions. Its structure is very different from one sector to another. For the different sectors, the origin of all income must be shown. Here for the companies, it also shows the income from the property. The balance of this account is the gross primary income balance (GIPS).

- ✓ **The Secondary Income Distribution Account**

It shows transfers related to income tax levies and social redistribution related to corporations. The balance is gross disposable income (GDI) (what can be spent once all statutory and contractual taxes have been paid).

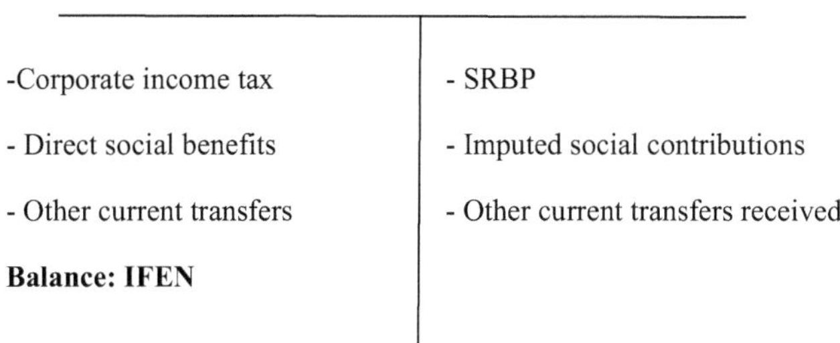

- ✓ **The Use of Income Account**

For non-financial enterprises or companies, consumption expenditure (CD) is equal to 0 because all consumption is intermediate consumption. Moreover, for non-financial corporations, Gross Savings is equal to Disposable Income (GDI). Its balance is Gross Savings (GS).

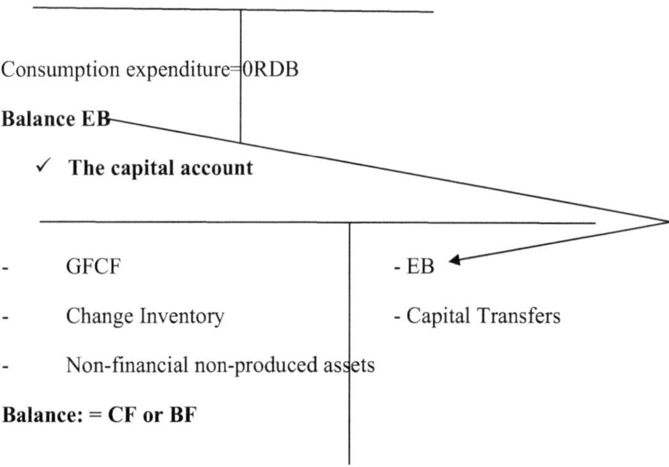

Its purpose is to show how savings and net transfers i.e. transfers received minus transfers paid out in capital are used for capital formation. This corresponds to the total resources that will be used to finance investment (I). The balance can be positive (financing capacity) or negative (financing requirement).

- ✓ **The financial account**

It is intended to describe all financial transactions between sectors, i.e. how the financing capacity has been used or how the financing need has been covered. This account contains only financial transactions.

2°). THE HOUSEHOLDS

- ✓ **Production account**

It is the same for all sectors. Here, for households, production will be mainly that of individual entrepreneurs. But households that are not individual entrepreneurs can also have a production activity. Example: production for own final use (PEFP).

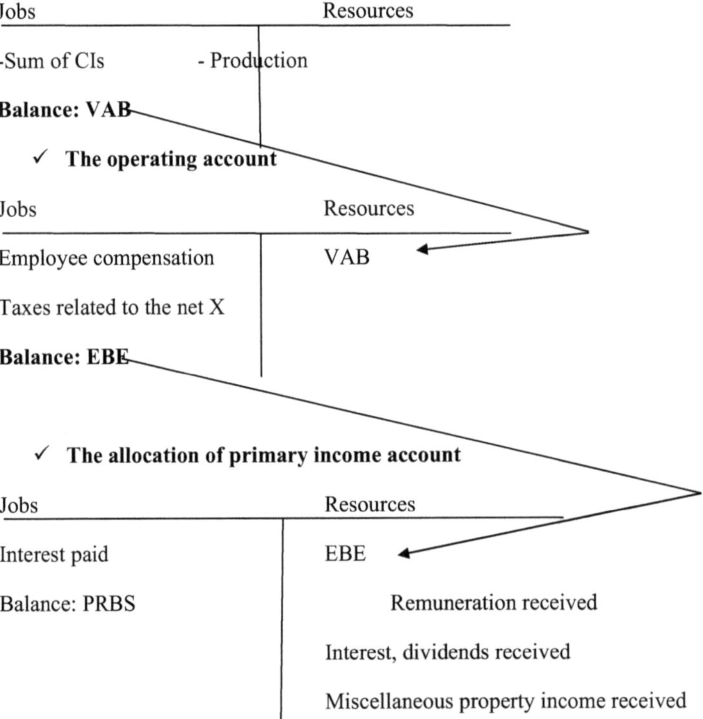

- ✓ **The Secondary Income Distribution Account**

The balance is equal to the IFEN. The GDI will go into the Utilization of Income Account for consumption and what will not be consumed will represent savings.

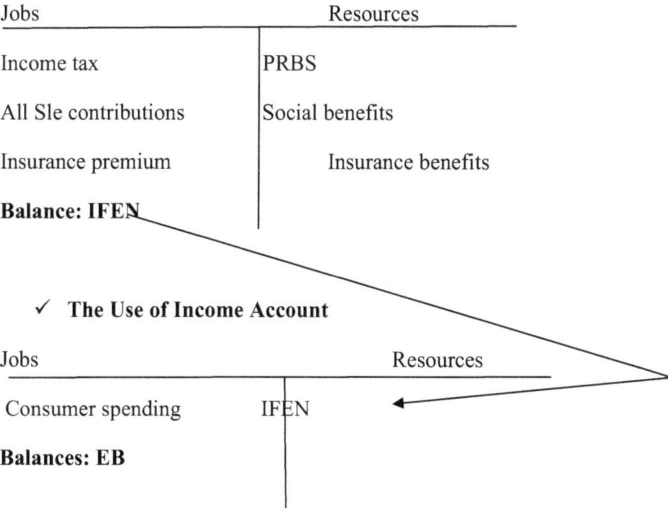

Jobs	Resources
Income tax	PRBS
All Sle contributions	Social benefits
Insurance premium	Insurance benefits
Balance: IFEN	

- ✓ **The Use of Income Account**

Jobs	Resources
Consumer spending	IFEN
Balances: EB	

- ✓ **The capital account and the financial account**

Both accounts are of the same type as the corporate account, except that for households (excluding sole proprietors), the only GFCF taken into account is the acquisition of housing.

3°) PUBLIC ADMINISTRATIONS

- ✓ **Production account**

Their production is non-market. It is valued on the basis of production costs. These consist of intermediate consumption (IC) + compensation of employees + taxes on production + consumption of fixed capital.

- ✓ **Operating account**

There are no changes. It is the same as for non-financial corporations or households.

- ✓ **Allocation of primary income account**

Jobs	Resources
Property income paid	EBE
	Tax at X° received - Expl. grant
	Property income received
Balance: PRBS	

- **Secondary Income Distribution Account**

Jobs	Resources
Social benefits	PRBS
Transfers to NPISHs	Income and wealth taxes
Balance: IFEN	Social security contributions
	Transfers received

- **Use of Income Account**

Here, consumption expenditure represents, by convention, the share of non-market production. This consumption expenditure is broken down into two items: individual consumption expenditure (the share of non-market services that have been consumed individually by households) and collective consumption expenditure (the share of indivisible non-market services consumed by the community).

Employment	Resource
DCRDB	
Balance: EB	

- **Capital Account**

This account has the same structure as before.

CHAPTER 3. PRESENTATION OF THE ECONOMY

The national accounts are based on two types of representation: tables (IOTs, EOTs) synthesising economic information (transactions in goods and services, distributive transactions, financial transactions) relating to the different institutional sectors; the economic circuit emphasising the different interdependencies between economic agents.

III.1 THE VARIOUS TABLES OF THE NATIONAL ACCOUNTS

National accounts summarize economic information in two tables. The input-output table gives a description of the interdependence between branches (product approach). The overall economic picture is a juxtaposition of the accounts of all institutional sectors (income approach).

1. The Input-Output Table (IOT)

All economic transactions on goods and services are reproduced in the *IOT* (Input-Output Table). The IOT is a table designed to describe the structure of national production. It is a double-entry table, presenting the resources of each branch in column and the uses of each product in line. The IOT also reflects the network of interdependencies that characterizes an economy at a given point in time. It is used to calculate GDP (Gross Domestic Product).

The constitution of this table is the fundamental basis for understanding national accounts. It is used to define the national productive structure, the balance of B&S in each branch.

On line, the IOT presents branches, which corresponds to the most aggregated level of the product nomenclature.

- The first table shows the total resources available to the economy for each product.

- The second table details the intermediate consumption sold by the branch to other branches. It is one of the interests of the TES to break down the intermediate consumption of the product between the different branches acquiring it.

- The third table shows the uses of the industry's output (other than intermediate consumption). If we aggregate the ICs, each line shows the resource-use balance for each of the branches.

Production (P) + Import (IMP)= CI (∑CI) + CF(∑CF) + GFCF ± VS + Export (EXP)

Schematically, the IOT is as follows:

Ressource en Production			Echange interindustriel						Demande Finale			
P	IMP	Σ	Branche						CF	FBCF	VS	EXP
				I	II	...	M	Σ				
Σ	Σ	Σ	Σ									

Production et Exportation					
Σ	I	II	...	M	Σ
Σ *CI*					
IMP					
VAB					
P					
Impôt					

2. <u>The Overall Economic Table (OEE)</u>

The EEO summarises all the flow accounts of the national accounts. The use of the TEE allows the analysis of recent and past economic activity. It is the matrix of the national accounts. Each column corresponds to the debit transactions or use and each line represents the credit or resource. The total of the credit or resource is equal to the total of the debit or use so that the sector accounts are balanced.

CHAPTER 4. GDP

4.1 CONCEPT ON MACROECONOMIC AGGREGATES

The aggregates are synthetic quantities that measure the outcome of economic activity of all resident sectors.

In order to measure economic activity, it will be necessary to define a number of macroeconomic variables called aggregates.

- *The added value*

Represents the additional value a company adds to its production. This value or wealth created during the production process corresponds to the different incomes allocated to the holders of the production factors made available to the company.

VA= Value of products - Values of intermediate consumption.

- *GDP at market price*: the latter makes it possible to assess the value of goods and services produced by national production from three angles: activity, output and expenditure.

Activity (production approach)	Product (demand approach)	Income (income approach)
Added value + Taxes on products - Subsidies on products	Final consumption expenditure + Gross fixed capital formation + Exports - Imports	Compensation of employees + Gross operating surplus + Taxes related to production and imports - Subsidies on production
GDP	GDP	GDP

However, in order to make some international comparisons, statisticians have had to calculate *Net Domestic Product* (NDP) and *Gross National Product* (GNP).

PIN	GNP
GDP - consumption of fixed capital	GDP + Labour, property and business income received from the rest of the world - Labour, property and business income paid to the rest of the world

- *National income at market prices* is the sum of income received by resident units and taxes related to production and imports, net of subsidies. It is identified with net national product. It is equal to (GDP at market price - consumption of fixed capital + labour, property and entrepreneurial income received from the rest of the world - labour, property and entrepreneurial income paid to the rest of the world). In national income at market prices, there are two separate components, the sum of primary income of resident units and taxes related to production and imports net of operating subsidies.

National factor income includes only income, so it is equal to (national income at market price - Taxes related to production and imports + operating subsidies). National factor income can be broken down into compensation of employees and property and business income.

- *Gross National Disposable Income* (GNDI) at market prices is calculated using three methods.

. GNDI = Σ of the gross disposable income of the different sectors (this is actually the balance of the income accounts)

. GNDI = National Final Consumption + Gross National Savings .

. GNDI = GDP + Current income of the rest of the world net of similar income paid to the rest of the world.

The examination of economic developments can be facilitated by calculating the ratios between two operations in the economic table.

The average propensity of	*The average propensity to save of*	*The household financial savings rate*	*The investment rate of non-financial SQS*

households to consume	*households or savings rate*		
Household final consumption/income household gross disposable income	Gross household savings/gross disposable income of households	Financing capacity/ Gross Disposable Income	GFCF/VA gross

4.2 VALUE ADDED AND GDP

The concept of added value makes it possible not to count the same good several times. Value added does not exactly represent the new value created in the production process by the industry. Wear and tear and obsolescence of capital are not, in fact, subtracted. Real value added, which is an indicator of value creation, should be net of wear and tear on capital, which is interpreted as a destruction of value, in the same way as intermediate consumption.

VAN = P - CI - CCF

With: NPV = net value added;

P= Production

CI= Intermediate consumption

CCF= Fixed Capital Consumption.

In practice, the national accounts do not integrate the CSW and prefer to keep the value added in its gross form, i.e. without subtracting consumption from fixed capital. It prefers to retain a definition of value that is too broad but correctly estimated, rather than a complete definition with a large margin of error.

GDP can be defined as the sum of VA produced in the economy. It is therefore identical to write :

GDP= CF + FBCF + VS + EXP - IMP

That is, GDP is equal to the sum of domestic demand and the external balance.

GDP can still be defined as all goods and services produced by resident units and made available for final consumption.

GDP = $\sum$P = $\sum$ (P - CI) = $\sum$ - $\sum$

GDP can be measured from three different but complementary perspectives: production approach, demand approach and income approach.

It consists of a market component and a non-market component. It is valued at current or constant price.

- ✓ **Evaluation of GDP at current prices**

It is the GDP of a year valued at the prices of the same year.

$$\textit{Nominal GDP}_n = Qn \times Pn$$

- ✓ **Valuation of GDP at constant prices**

This assessment eliminates the price increase (inflation) between two periods and measures the actual or real "enrichment" of the country (real GDP or Volume GDP).

- Valuation at base year prices

That is to say, the real GDP of year n at year n-m prices is written as follows:

Real GDPn x Pricen-m=Qn x Pm

Example: Real GDP 2007 at 2000 prices will be Real GDP $_{07}$ *x Price* $_{00}$ = *Q07 x P00*

- GDP price index (GDP deflator)

$$\text{Price index} = \frac{PIB\ en\ valeur_n}{PIB\ réel_{n-m}\ x\ Prix_{n-1}} = \frac{Q_n\ x\ P_n}{Q_{n-m}\ x\ P_{n-1}}$$

- GDP volume index

Increases in quantities (volume) produced. It is equal to the ratio of real GDP in year n valued at base year (n-m) prices to GDP in value in year (n-m).

$$\text{Volume index} = \frac{PIB\ réel_n\ x\ Prix_{n-m}}{PIB\ Valeur_{n-m}} = \frac{Q_n\ x\ P_{n-m}}{Q_{n-m}\ x\ P_{n-m}}$$

Here, (n-m) represents the base year.

n represents the evaluation year.

CHAPTER 5. BALANCE OF PAYMENTS

1.1 GENERAL PRINCIPLES

1.1.1 Definition

The balance of payments is a statistical document, presented according to the rules of double-entry accounting, which compiles and orders all economic transactions with the rest of the world during a given period.

Despite its name, the balance of payments is no longer intended to report payments but transactions between residents and non-residents.

It is a balanced balance, with each transaction with a non-resident having a financial counterpart, a change in assets or liabilities vis-à-vis residents.

1.1.2 Objective

At the national level, the balance of payments makes it possible to assess the country's integration into its external environment and constitutes an essential element of the national accounts by providing the statistical elements that contribute to the compilation of national aggregates (GDP, National Income, International Commitments, etc.).

The IMF, which is responsible under its Articles of Agreement for ensuring the smooth functioning of the international monetary system, has been entrusted with the task of standardizing concepts, definitions, classifications and conventions to facilitate the collection, presentation and comparison of balance of payments statistics at the national and international levels.

1.1.3 Unit of account and valuation principles

The balance of payments shall be drawn up in national currency. Foreign currency transactions are reported in the original currency and are then translated at the monthly average exchange rate of the currency concerned against the national currency.

For flows calculated on the basis of stocks at the beginning and end of the period, the change in stocks during the period is carried out in the original currency and then this change is translated on the basis of the monthly average exchange rate of the currency in question against the national currency.

1.1.4 Concepts

a. Residents/Non-Residents

The basic criterion is that of the residence of the economic agents, distinct from the nationality criterion. For balance of payments purposes, residents and non-residents are defined as follows:

1°. Residents

- Natural persons having their main centre of interest in the DRC, whatever their nationality, with the exception of foreign civil servants and military personnel posted in the DRC who remain non-residents.
- Congolese civil servants and other public officials posted abroad or placed at the disposal of international organisations and other non-resident employers.
- Legal persons, Congolese or foreign, for their establishments in the DRC, with the exception of representations of foreign countries and international organisations established in the DRC, when there is a real economic activity carried out in the DRC by autonomous production units, whatever their legal form (subsidiary, branch, agency, office, etc.).

2°. Non-Residents

- Foreign or Congolese natural persons who habitually live abroad, i.e. who have their actual place of residence there, with the exception of Congolese representations and Congolese officials posted abroad.
- Legal persons, foreign or Congolese, for their establishments abroad where there is a real economic activity carried out abroad by equally autonomous production units.

b. Resident Economic Sectors

In some parts of the balance of payments, notably current transfers, portfolio investment and other investment, the amounts recorded are classified according to the economic sector to which the residents party to the transaction belong. A distinction is made in this case between :

- The monetary authority, i.e. the Central Bank;
- The general government sector ;
- The MFI sector comprises resident credit institutions and all other resident financial institutions whose business is to receive deposits and/or close substitutes for deposits from entities other than MFIs and which, for their own account, grant credits and/or make investments in securities.
- Other sectors", which record transactions by economic agents other than those included in the three previous sectors: industrial and commercial enterprises, insurance, non-monetary financial institutions, including investment firms and non-monetary investment funds, non-profit institutions serving households, and households.

c. Maturity: long term/short term

For balance of payments purposes, the long term corresponds to an original maturity of more than one year; the short term corresponds to an original maturity of one year or less.

1.1.5 The Data Collection System

The collection of balance of payments data is based, for the most part, on the requirement for all residents to report to the central bank their transactions with the non-resident, either directly or through resident banks.

Transactions are generally reported in terms of gross flows, with revenue and expenditure netted. However, movements in the external assets and liabilities of the central bank, general government, credit institutions and investment firms, as well as those in trade credits and reserve assets, are the result of changes between the debit and end-of-period stocks.

1.2 REPORTING AGENTS

1.2.1 Credit institutions

They report:

- payments made, for their own account or on behalf of their resident customers, to non-residents in respect of trade in services, income, current and capital transfers, direct investment and non-bank lending and borrowing.

  The payment report shall provide details on the economic nature of the transaction, the country of counterparty, the amount and currency of the transaction, and the resident identification number.

- Securities transactions between residents and non-residents. These flows are reported on a security-by-security basis.
- Outstanding bank deposits and loans vis-à-vis non-residents. Credit institutions report their outstanding amounts by type of counterparty (interbank and financial customers, non-financial customers) and currency of operation, with a distinction between long-term and short-term.

1.2.2 The Central Bank

It manages the State's foreign exchange reserves in accordance with the rules laid down by law and reports the amounts outstanding. The transactions of its customers or of the State on the Treasury account follow the same reporting principles as those carried out by the banking sector for its customers.

1.2.3 public accountants

They transmit information on their settlement with foreign countries, the main declarants include, the foreign payment houses, ...

1.2.4 Investment Companies

They report their outstanding cash, receivables and commitments with foreign countries.

1.2.5 Customs

The customs administration transmits data on exports and imports of goods to the central bank.

1.2.6 The Households

In addition to the declarations that they may be required to make for partial direct reporting, households are likely to respond to surveys conducted by an external service provider to enable the Balance of Payments Directorate to feed the flows under the heading "travel" for personal or professional reasons.

1.2.7 Others

There are other reporting agents that can help provide information for the balance of payments. These include :

- *General direct reporters*: are enterprises or groups of enterprises whose transactions with foreign countries, whatever their nature or modalities, exceed, during a calendar year, for at least one service or income item of the balance of payments, an amount fixed by decree. They report all cross-border transactions, including flows via foreign accounts and clearing houses. One exception is that portfolio investment related to liquidity management and capital income, when carried out via resident banks, need not be reported; it is up to the banks involved to do so.

- *Foreign airlines*: operating in the DRC declare the regulations related to their commercial activity of stopover or representation, as well as operations with their head office or with sister companies abroad.

- *Economic interest groups issuing payment cards* : (Visa, Eurocard, American Express, Diners) declare cash withdrawals and payments made for the purchase of services by non-residents in the DRC or by residents abroad, via a payment card. These declarations are detailed by country, by type of card (personal or professional) and by type of transaction (ATM withdrawals, internet payments, other payments).

1.3 THE STRUCTURE AND HEADINGS OF THE BALANCE OF PAYMENTS

1.3.1 The Structure

There are four scale structures:

1°. Trade Balance

Clears a balance, especially the trade balance. It includes sales and purchases of goods as well as international negotiations (commission-based trading transactions).

2°. Balance of the invisible

It records transactions relating to services, consisting mainly of :

- Transport, insurance, management services, banking services ;
- Patents, licenses;

- Unilateral transfers (donations, transfers of savings from resident foreign workers and nationals abroad) ;
- Sightseeing.

3°. Balance of capital

Traces mainly acquisitions of non-financial assets (e.g. purchases and sales of patents).

4°. Balance of financial accounts

Includes all trade credits, financial investments and direct investments abroad. Four groups can be distinguished :

- Trade credits, which are loans linked to sales;
- Ordinary loans and credits ;
- In particular, direct investment abroad for the purpose of establishing a foreign subsidiary, buying a foreign company or acquiring an equity stake in a foreign company.
- Portfolio investments (transactions in securities) which are investments in creations, bonds without the acquisition of a majority holding.

For each of the balances, uses are recorded on the debit side and include all relative exports, while resources are recorded on the credit side and include all relative imports.

It should be noted that the trade balance and the balance of invisibles give the current account balance, the balance of invisibles is the result of the balance of services and the current transfer balance.

The nation's financing capacity (balance +) or need (balance -) is the result of the current and capital account balance, while the financing capacity or need and the financial account balance make up the balance of payments.

1.3.2 Balance of Payments Headings

Schematically, these headings can be presented as follows:

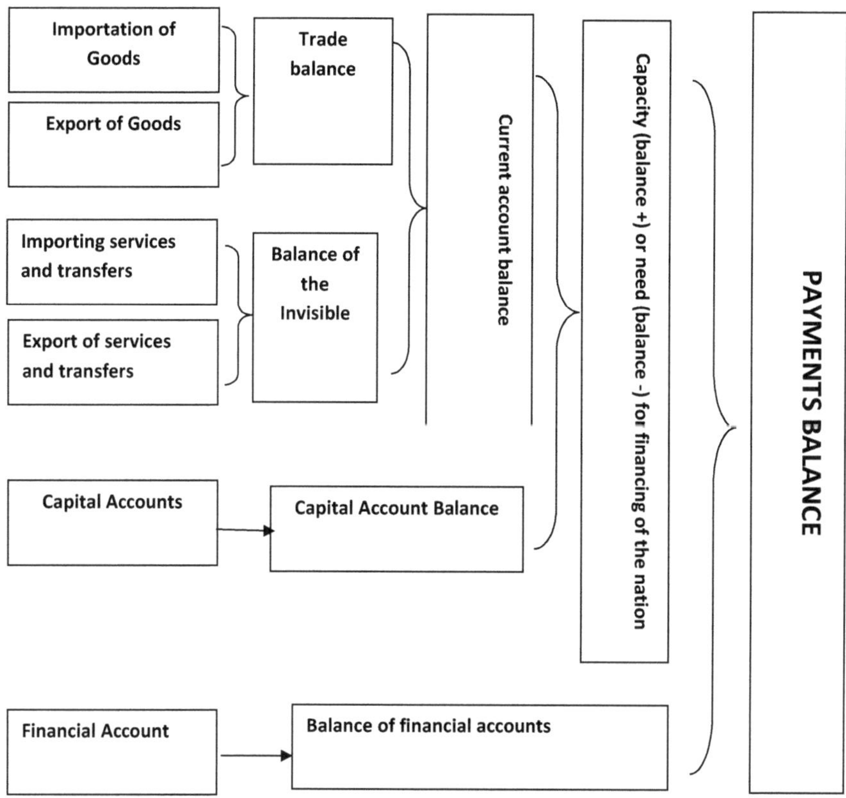

NATIONAL ACCOUNTS

EXERCISES AND RESOLUTIONS

Question 1.

Consider a simple economy that produces only one final good that is not used in the production of other goods: the shirt. The three other goods produced are intermediate goods, as they are used in the manufacture of the shirt, directly or indirectly. They are wool, yarn and fabric.

Let us also assume that this economy has no government, so there are no taxes, no subsidies, and no economic relations with foreign countries, hence no imports and exports. The main activities for the production of the shirt are: breeding, spinning, weaving and tailoring. Each activity uses labour and therefore pays wages. Each of them generates profits. Breeding is of a particular type here. It is transhumant or nomadic, the sheep finding their water and grass in abundance, without intermediate costs for the farmer. The latter is limited to paying shepherds and making profits from the sale of wool.

From the above, the farm supports 3 Fc for the payment of wages and winds its wool at 8 Fc. The spinning mill buys wool at 8 Fc to produce yarn. This activity supports 3 Fc for wages. After the production it sells the yarn at 16 Fc. In order to produce fabrics, it buys yarns and pays wages at 3 Fc. After production we sell fabrics at 25 Fc. To make shirts, we pay wages at 10 Fc and we buy fabrics. Finally we sell our shirt, which is our finished product, for 40 Fc.

TD.

- Open a debit-credit account for each of the four production activities taking place in the country.
- Calculate the value added of each of four activities and determine the GDP.

Solution

Elevage		Filage		Tissage		Confection	
Débit	***Crédit***	***Débit***	***Crédit***	***Débit***	***Crédit***	***Débit***	***Crédit***
Salaire 3	Laine 8	Laine 8 Salaire 3	Filage 16	Fil 16 Salaire 3	Tissus 25	Tissus 25 salaire 10	Chemise 40
Profit 5		***Profit 5***		***Profit 6***		***Profit 5***	
Total 8	**total 8**	**Total 16**	**Total 16**	**Total 25**	**Total 25**	**Total 40**	**Total 40**
VA= 8		***VA= 16-8=8***		***VA=25-16=9***		***VA=40-25=15***	

PIB= ∑ VA=8+8+9+15=40 Fc

Question 2.

Consider a nation provisionally made up of the following entities: Businesses, Households and Government.

- Businesses sell goods and services worth 14 million to households and 18 million to general government. In addition, firms pay 35 million wages to households and 10 million in taxes to general government.
- Finally, the general government also pays 22 million wages to households and receives 15 million in taxes from them.

TD.

- Present the following operations in the overall economic picture (TEE)
- Present the global account of each agent.

Solution

- ***TEE***

	Entreprise	Ménage	Admin. Pub	Total Ress.
Entreprise		14	18	**32**
Ménage	35		22	**57**
Admin. Pub	10	15		**25**
Total Emploi	**45**	**29**	**40**	**114**

- Global Account

We note that the State has a budget deficit of 15 billion FC and the Enterprise has a financing need of 13 billion FC. Therefore, the household has the financial capacity to finance the State and the Enterprise (15+13=28). These operations take place on the financial market.

Compte des Entreprises			
Salaires versés aux ménages	35	Vente des biens et services : 14+18	32
Impôts payés	10	**Solde: Besoin de Finacement**	**13**
Total	45	Total	45

Comptes des Ménages			
Achats biens et services	14	salaires recus 35+22	57
impôt payé à l'administration publique	15		
Solde: Capacité de financement	**28**		
Total	57	Total	57

Compte de l'Administration Publique			
Achats Biens et services	18	Impôts reçus 10+15	25
Salaires payés aux ménages	22	**Solde: Besoin de financement**	**15**
Total	40	Total	40

Question 3.

Consider an economy with four economic agents: households, businesses, government and the rest of the world.

0. Households consumed goods and services (**C**) of CF 900 million. They paid taxes (**TM**) amounting to CF 150 million.
1. Firms made investments (**I**) in the order of Fc 318 million; paid salaries to households (**WE**) of Fc 720 million and paid indirect taxes and social contributions to the State (**TE**) of Fc 480 million. These enterprises produced (**P**) worth 1500.
2. The State made public investments (**G**) of about 270 million and paid out to households income in terms of civil servants' salaries, social benefits and allowances (**WA**) of 390 million Fc.
3. The rest of the world observed exports (**X**) amounting to CF 321 million and imports (**M**) of CF 309 million.

TD.

Present the above data in the form of the economic circuit, considering that all transactions take place in the market for goods and services.

Solution

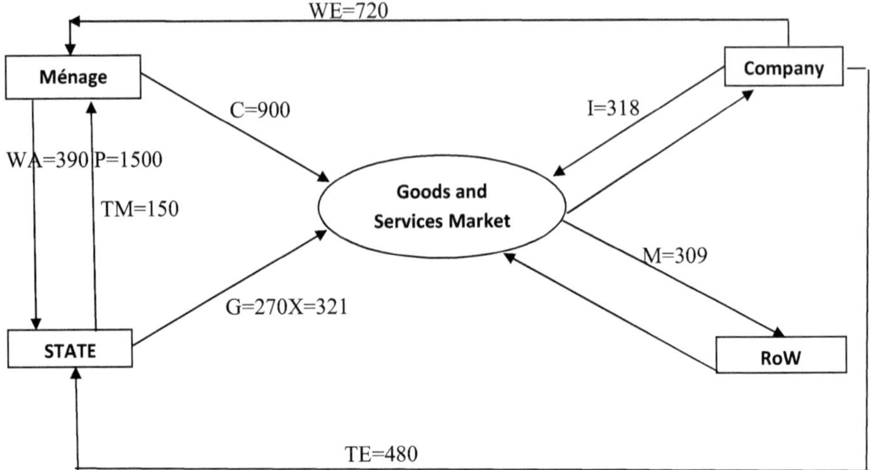

Question 4.

Or an economy reduced to four branches. The agriculture branch produces product 1, the industrial branch produces product 2, the market service branch produces product 3 and the non-market service branch produces product 4.

The following information is given:

- Intra-consumption is 14 in agriculture, 582 in industry, 528 in market services and 6 in non-market services.
- The intermediate consumption of Agriculture in products 2 and 3 are respectively 24 and 6. Those of industry in product 1, 3 and 4 are 36,182 and 5 respectively. Those of market services in products 1, 2 and 4 are 2,156 and 9 respectively. Those of non-market services in product 1, 2 and 3 are of the order of 1, 54 and 57. There is no other intermediate consumption.
- The productions of the branches are of the order of 89, 1570, 1355, 444.
- Imports in product 1 are worth 9, those in product 2 are worth 420 and those in product 3 are worth 66. There are no other imports.
- Exports are in the order of 11, 378, 59 and 1.
- The final consumption of households in agriculture is 30, in industry 479, in market services 455 and 48 in non-market services. Those of the administration are in the same order: 0, 28, 39, 355.

- The investments made by agriculture are 1, those made by industry are 287 and those made by market service are 90. Non-market services did not make investments.
- Inventory was varied in product 1 and 2 only for a value of 3 and 2 respectively.

TD.

Construct the IOT and determine the GDP according to the production approach.

Solution

	Ressource			Echange inter secteur						Demandes Finales				
	P	***IMPORT***	***Tot***		***Agri***	***Indu***	***SM***	***SNM***	***Tot***	***CFM***	***CFA***	***FBCF***	***VS***	***EXPO***
1	89	9	98	***Agri***	14	36	2	1	53	30	0	1	3	11
2	1570	420	1990	***Indu***	24	582	156	54	816	479	28	287	2	378
3	1355	66	1421	***SM***	6	182	528	57	773	455	39	90	0	59
4	444	0	444	***SNM***	0	5	9	6	20	48	355	0	0	1
Tot	3458	495	3953		44	805	695	118	1662					
				Production et Exploitation										
				Tot CI	44	805	695	118						
				Produc	89	1570	1355	444	**PIB**					
				VAB	45	765	660	326	**1796**					

Question 5.

An Economy produces and consumes bread and cars. The prices of a car were 50000 in 2000 and 60000 in 2010. The price of a unit of bread was 10 in 2000 and 20 in 2010. The number of cars produced was 100 in 2000 and 120 in 2010. The number of bread units produced is 500000 in 2000 and 400000 in 2010.

TD

Using the year 2000 as a benchmark, calculate nominal GDP, real GDP and the GDP deflator. Then take 2010 as the base year.

Solution

PIB nominal=	(50000x100)+(10x500000)=	10000000	(en 2000)
	(60000x120)+(20x400000)=	15200000	(en 2010)

PIB réel=	(50000x100)+(10x500000)=	10000000	(en 2000, en prix de 2000)
	(50000x120)+(10x400000)=	10000000	(en 2010, en prix de 2000)
	(60000x100)+(20x500000)=	16000000	(en 2000, en prix de 2010)
	(60000x120)+(20x400000)=	15200000	(en 2010, en prix de 2010)

Déflateur PIB=	15200000/10000000 =	1,52	(En prénant comme base 2000)
	10000000/16000000 =	0,625	(en prénant comme base 2010)

Comments :

Taking the year 2000 as a benchmark, real GDP remains stable. Taking 2010 as a reference, GDP declines by 5%. The GDP deflator indicates that there was a 52% increase from 2000 to 2010 using 2000 as the base. And using 2010 as a base, GDP increased by 60% from 2000 to 2010.

Here the GDP deflator is given by the formula : $\frac{PIBno\min al}{PIBréel}$

Question 6.

Suppose that the year 2015 had the following transaction flows :

- Individuals purchased $146.5 billion worth of daily consumer goods and services from local businesses (EC) and travelled abroad, spending $2.5 billion. Individuals paid direct taxes of CF 44 billion.
- Firms paid these same individuals $180 billion in wages, interest and dividends (WD).
- The state paid 25 billion to those working in the civil service (GW).
- The companies also sold 8.2 billion (GBP) worth of daily consumer goods to the state and exported 52 billion goods and services (E).
- Two other external revenues of the country were the repatriation of salaries by nationals working abroad for an amount of 0.7 billion (TRP) and budgetary aid granted by a foreign government to the central administration for an amount of 0.3 billion (TRPU).
- The government collected 11 billion in income taxes (TDE) and 8.5 billion in indirect taxes net of subsidies, including customs taxes (TI), from companies. It also had to make interest payments on its debt: 1.5 and 2 billion were paid respectively to companies (INTE) and individuals (INTM), while interest on external debt rose to 6.8 billion (INTR).

- The rest of the world sold 53.5 billion goods and services (ME) to companies and received 0.5 billion factor income (RF) from them, mainly profits made by foreign firms located in the country, part of these profits having been repatriated to the country of origin of these same firms.
- Finally, all enterprises, individuals and the State made investments in the form of equipment purchases, new construction and infrastructure works, which amounted to 47 billion (I), if we include the increases in inventories of raw materials and semi-finished products.

TD :

1. Introducing the EEO
2. Present the agents' global accounts.

Solution

1. TEE

	Entreprise	Particuliers	Etat	Reste du M	Accum. Cap	Total Ress
Entreprise		CE (146,5)	GB(8,2),INT E(1,5)	E(52)	I(47)	255,2
Particulier	WD(180)		GW(25),INT M(2)	TRP(0,7)		207,7
Etat	TI(8,5), TDE(11)	TM(44)		TRPU(0,3)		63,8
Reste du Mo	ME(53,5),RF (0,5)	MM(2,5)	INTR(6,8)			63,3
Accum Capit	SE(1,7)	SM(14,7)	SG(20,3)	SR(10,3)		47
Total emploi	255,2	207,7	63,8	63,3	47	0

2. **Agent Account**

COMPTE DES ENTREPRISES

Débit	Montant	Crédit	Montant
salaires, intérêt et dividendes payé (WD)	180,00	Achats par les ménages (CE)	146,50
Impôts indirects (TI)	8,50	Achats par l'Etat (GB)	8,20
Impôts directs (TDE)	11,00	Exportation B&S non facteur	52,00
Importation des B&S non facteurs (ME)	53,50	Invsetissements ou FBCF (I)	47,00
Revenus des facteurs payés au RM (RF)	0,50	Intérêts de la dette de l'Etat (INTE)	1,50
Epargne des entreprises (SE)	1,70		
Total	255,20	Total	255,20

COMPTE DES PARTICULIERS

Débit	Montant	Crédit	Montant
Achats aux entreprises (CE)	146,50	Salaires, intérêt et dividendes (WD)	180,00
Impôts directs ™	44,00	Salaires administratifs (GW)	25,00
Depenses à l'étranger (MM)	2,50	Intérêt de la dette de l'Etat (INTM)	2,00
Eparge des particuliers (SE)	14,70	Rapatriement salaire par le RdM (TRP)	0,70
Total	207,70	Total	207,70

COMPTE DE L'ETAT

Débit	Montant	Crédit	Montant
Achats par l'Etat aux entreprises (GB)	8,20	impôts indirects net (TI)	8,50
Salaires administratifs (GW)	25,00	Impôts directs payés par les entreprise	11,00
Intérêts payés aux entreprises (INTE)	1,50	Impôts directs payés par les particulier	44,00
Intérêts payés particuliers (INTM)	2,00	Aide budgétaires (TRPU)	0,30
Intérêts payés au reste du monde (INTR)	6,80		
Eparge de l'Etat (SG)	20,30		
Total	63,80	Total	63,80

COMPTE DU RESTE DU MONDE

Débit	Montant	Crédit	Montant
Exportation des B&S non facteurs	52,00	Importation des B&S no facteur	53,50
Rapatriements de salaires au pays (TRP)	0,70	Dépanses des visiteurs (MM)	2,50
Aide budgétaire accordée à l'Etat (TRPU)	0,30	Revenus de facteurs payés (RF)	0,50
Eparge étrangere (SR)	10,30	Intérêts de la dette extérieure payé	6,80
Total	63,30	Total	63,30

COMPTE D'ACCUMULATION DU CAPITAL

Débit	Montant	Crédit	Montant
FBCF de la nation	47,00	Eparge des entreprises (SE)	1,70
		Eparge des particuliers (SM)	14,70
		Epargne de l'Etat (SG)	20,30
		Epargne etrangère (SR)	10,30
Total	47,00	Total	47,00

Question 7.

Or an economy reduced to 3 branches: branch I produces product 1, branch II produces product 2 and branch III produces product 3.

The following information is given:

Intra-branch I consumption is 20, branch II consumption is 50 and branch III consumption is 25.

The intermediate consumption of branch I in product 2 and 3 are 10 and 0 respectively, those of branch II in product 1 and 3 are 100 and 200 respectively and those of branch III in product 1 and 2 are 80 and 10 respectively.

The productions of branches I, II, and III are in the order of 100, 500, and 200.

Branch I pays 20 in compensation of wages; branches II and III pay 50 and 15 respectively in compensation of wages.

Taxes related to production are in the same order 5, 30, 10.

Imports in product 1 are worth 300, those in product 2 are worth 100 and those in product 3 are worth 100.

Exports are in the same order 0, 30, 25.

The fixed consumption of product 1 is 120, that of product 2 is 150 and that of product 3 is 25.

TD

Knowing that inventory changes are in the order 20, 50, 0, we ask to construct the IOT and verify the GDP according to the 3 optics (expenditure optic, production optic, income optic).

Solutions

Note:

We know that GDP is calculated by the following formula (according to each perspective)

GDP=∑CF+∑FBCF+∑VS+∑EXP-∑IMP (expenditure perspective)

GDP=∑VAB (production perspective)

GDP=∑RS+∑Impôt+∑EBE (income perspective)

Gold VAB= RS+ Tax+ EBE And therefore EBE=VAB-RS-Tax

	Ressource			Echange entre secteur				Demande Finale				
	Prod	*Import*	*Σ*	*I*	*II*	*III*	*Σ*	*CF*	*FBCF*	*VS*	*Export*	*Σ*
1	100	300	400	20	100	80	200	120	60	20	0	200
2	500	100	600	10	50	10	70	150	300	50	30	530
3	200	100	300	0	200	25	225	25	25	0	25	75
Σ	800	500	1300	30	350	115	495	295	385	70	55	805

Production et exploitation

CI	30	350	115
RS	20	50	15
Impôt	5	30	10
EBE	45	70	60
IMPOR	300	100	100
Production	100	500	200
VA	70	150	85

PIB=	305 (optique dépense)
PIB=	305 (Optique production)
PIB=	305 (Optique revenu)

Question 8.

That is to say the economy of the DRC with the elements of the accounts of economic agents on 31/12/2015 (in millions of FC).

1. Purchase of PMs abroad by companies 100
2. Purchase of consumer goods by the State 50
3. Export of the nation 100
4. Sale of consumer B&S by companies 150 000
5. Salary received from companies 60
6. Corporate income tax 20 000
7. Household income tax 40 000
8. Importing the nation 140 000
9. Salaries received from the State 70 000
10. Sale of production goods 800
11. State subsidy to companies 30 000
12. Household Transfers Abroad 500
13. Household contribution 200
14. Corporate interests in the State 400
15. State subsidy to companies 10

16. Transfer from the rest of the world to business 15 000

17. Transfer from the rest of the world to the household 25.

TD

- Open the global accounts of the sectors and check the equality of capacity of one to the financing needs of the other.
- Present these operations in the form of the TEE

Printed by Books on Demand GmbH, Norderstedt / Germany